GLASS HEART AND TIGERS EYE: THE POWER IN VULNERABILITY

Emri

BookLeaf
Publishing

India | USA | UK

Glass Heart and Tigers Eye: The power in vulnerability

© 2021 Remi Carolyne (Emri)

Presentation by BookLeaf Publishing

Web: www.bookleafpub.com

E-mail: info@bookleafpub.com

ISBN: 9789358739350

First edition 2021

DEDICATION AND PREFACE

I started writing as a way to process my emotions and experiences of mental illness, and throughout this time I have to extend my deepest gratitude and thanks to my friends and family who have stood by me through the hardest times of my life.

I dedicated this book to allowing life to be what it is. We don't need to shape every life experience as a positive, a life lesson or something to grow from. Sometimes the best we can do for ourselves is to sit with our pain, feel it, and find a way to move with it and through it.

It's a cliché to say you aren't alone, but while all our experiences may be different, we've shared similar feelings, fears, joys. Remember you don't have to do anything alone, you aren't mean to live alone, recover alone. Connection and community is important, take time for just you when you need to, but please don't ever think you have to walk your path alone. You don't, and you shouldn't.

If you read this book, I hope you are able to take something from it, and if you do, I'd love to know what.

- Emri Collections / Remi Carolyne

I wanted the first thing I write to be beautiful, loving, hopeful.

But instead I feel like I'm sitting in the bottom of a deep dark well -

it's raining and the water is rising.

I can swim, but for how long?

And the question remains -

Do I even want to swim?

That is, do I really believe I can rise from this?

The water is rising

and I'm not as strong as I used to be.

That person feels like a ghost;

haunting me to remind me of everything I have lost,

or let go of.

The water is cold and so dark,

as if no amount of light could ever penetrate it to show what's truly
beneath the surface -

Yet it feels so familiar to me

like an old friend I've tried desperately to turn away from

but is always around the next corner,

waiting for me with a disturbed plastered grin.

The water is rising and I can't touch the bottom.

There was a time I could've confidently tread the depths until I
could crawl out the top -

Determined, strong willed and ready to

dance in the rain.

But the water is rising and I am tired.

I'm in the dark,

I'm cold,

I'm alone -

and it would be so easy to just

allow myself to submerge.

"I've got you babe"

Isn't what the strong, brave and protective male saviour tells me.

He is not the champion of this story;

really barely a side character.

His hold, control, is as weak as a breeze

failing to blow away a plastic bag.

"I've got you babe"

Is what I say to myself

as I stand from the dirt and thistles,

brushing myself down with torn finger tips...

I don't even flinch as my skins tears anew

under the pressure of my own determination

to get back up.

"I've got you babe"

I write in the steamed glass of the shower

as I wash away the grime, the blood, the pain.

Watch it swirl down the drain at my feet;

a dirty cloud

As I stand up taller and breathe in deeper,

tilting my head toward the light shining through the window.

"I've got you babe"

Is what I say to myself –

Because it is me who is strong, brave, and protective.

I am my saviour, I am my hero,

I am what makes me whole.

To have me, babe –

You better offer me something

I cannot provide myself.

To have me, babe –

You better add to my life what I cannot source myself –

what makes my muscles ease,

my stomach and chest pang,

my head tilt as I exhale.

My eyes close and my mind a perfectly blank slate.

Then,

and only then,

can you have me

Babe.

This is my time.

This is my moment to put myself first:

To allow myself to stop, breathe, and recognised my own needs...

and meet them.

Yet here I am,

with this fear deep in my stomach that I don't deserve it.

I don't deserve comfort, love or connection unless I've met other people's needs first.

I'm pushing a boulder up a hill,

Arms stretched out as I grit my teeth, sweat, and ache with its weight.

but this boulder is mine:

This is saying "no" to what hurts me,

saying "yes" to what gives me breath instead of starving me of oxygen, allowing myself to feel joy and pleasure without guilt or shame,

feeling the fear and doing it anyway;

It is everything I am fighting for.

Sometimes I slip or pause

because learning to self prioritise and not just sound assertive
requires a lot of energy.

I can take my time as I build my strength,

But as I push forward the grass is getting greener,

the birds chirp louder,

the breeze blows gently,

The flowers bloom and pass just to sprout new seed.

Maybe I'll be pushing the boulder forever;

but God is it worth it to feel this kind of freedom growing.

Where there is love there is oxygen.

It should never feel suffocating,

or have everything pinned to that one feeling,

one person.

Love is fundamental to life;

pleasure, calm, safety, comfort, connection.

But it isn't found in others;

rather it's how we experience ourselves alongside others.

I want to hold your hand in mind

and not just feel your skin,

but the vibration between us harmonising.

Oxygen that was always there,

becoming noticeable.

Love is always here;

floating around us,

invisible to the eye

but felt in the heart.

I set myself on fire

just to keep you warm,

and you complained I didn't burn brightly enough

to light your own way

through your own life.

I turned my volume down and held my breath,

so that you could not feel

guilt, pressure or real responsibility

when I needed help because of your ineptitude.

I tried to protect myself,

and you made a point

of digging me a deeper grave.

The reason you have nothing of your past to hold onto,

is because you threw it all away.

Now watch me light my own way,

but not by burning myself;

by lighting a torch.

Wrap your hand around my waist

and whisper in my ear.

Hold me like you know me

And I feel the heat of your fingers on my skin.

A wave of contentment takes over

and I know, just know

as surely as I breathe in this moment

I don't need to always be looking over my shoulder

for the next pain to smack me.

Wrap your hand around my throat

and call me by my name.

Choke me like you love me

Hold me so my eyes meet yours

and I feel my heartbeat in my temples

I trust you the way I trust

that the sun will always rise.

Breathe with me

and let what is constricting you go.

Miss me like you need me

Because you can know, just know

I am always going to be here

so we can watch the clouds in the sky

and the leaves on the trees change from green to orange and red.

The world may keep spining

and time may keep ticking

but as surely as the ocean licks the edges of the rocks along the beach,

We will always have this.

Sometimes the best way to create a new future is to do whatever
you need to survive.

My body is a collection of

paper cut outs from magazines

A collage of colours, misshapen pieces, and bad glue.

Where one piece ends another begins,

and those are my scars.

Millions of paper cut outs line this

body, mind, heart and soul.

And so millions of scars I have collected.

Each line and join a mark of my survival.

Sometimes I lose perspective,

But I always come back to looking up.

Where the glue may fade out

lose its stick,

I collect a new piece

because I don't hide my growth,

I don't hide my pain.

I survive and I am learning to thrive.

I am always waiting for the other shoe to drop,

for the shattering pain to follow the inexplicable pleasure.

It's not just that I'm pessimistic –

I hold a lot of hope.

It is that the joys, pleasures, comforts, and safety

have so frequently been short lived,

always a disruption splitting me from

what makes me breathe.

Inhale

but I do not want to hold my breath.

I want to exhale

as I feel the breeze on my skin and hear the falling of the rain on the rooftop.

If I shiver, I know I can get warm again...

It's just how long do I have to stand the blistering cold?

Will the other shoe always drop, though?

Life happens in ebbs and flows.

Maybe I just need the flows

to last longer.

We are taught to be fear the dark.

In the dark is what we have yet to recognise or experience and that
is what scares us.

In our minds run our fears and pains without

restraint, pause, or any true direction.

Impossible to turn off

and so easy to consider truthful

creating its own system of stories and beliefs.

The true scariest of things

are in front of us, surrounding us, in the light.

They are so clear and so present; we forget they are even there.

That is what makes them the most dangerous.

In the light is the familiar fears.

We know what they look like, how they hurt us, what they can do
to us –

So instead of standing in the shadow for a moment of potential new
pleasures,

we stay with the familiar ugly, the familiar pain, suffocate ourselves
slowly.

See what happens:

Close your eyes or even

Turn off the light.

Clever lines and empty words are one in the same.

Are they intentional lies or stumbled mistruths?

I am not sure I will ever have the answer.

Ultimately, does it really matter?

The only real difference is whether it was malicious or not –

The end result is still the same pain.

But I still wish I knew.

It was not love lacking that made the exit sign glow –

It was the falsehoods, broken promises, misleading monologues

Pressure to grin and bear it like I am on a cliffs edge

silently screaming, hoping and begging I wil fall to end the infinite
whirl-wind of love and death by one thousand tiny cuts.

Loving me like you hate me.

If one can call that crippling pedestal love.

The best thing I ever did

was leap off the pedestal.

22

I spent so long shrinking myself down

to fit into a perfect little box,

I fractured my mind from my body

and my body from my soul

because there was no single box

big enough

to fit all of me.

So ripped and torn,

I have been scattered across the galaxy.

I try to operate as one cohesive system

but control is an illusion and I'm continuing

to tear myself down into

smaller and

smaller pieces.

When did the space I allow myself to take up become so small?

Reclaiming my space -

allowing my mind, body and soul

to expand again takes patience and grit.

With the force of my inhale of breath,

I cast out my lines and hooks to pull myself together again.

Some parts I'll never get back

and while I may mourn the losses,

I exhale deeply and create new space for growth.

 Like a doll that has outgrown her house,

I feel too big for this place, this space.

My muscles ache as I'm squashed into a box I do not belong in.

Society likes to put us in categories and boxes -

But what happens when you don't fit just one?

When you grow,

but the box does not.

We fracture.

We tear ourselves apart to squeeze into spaces we never belonged
in in the first place.

stilted and sore,

beaten and bruised,

misplaced and misused,

this isn't what we should call home.

But how do we find home

in a society that was never made for us to grow?

The only way out is through –

Specifically, we must break through.

Tear apart the walls holding us,

scream into the crowd that spies us,

and make society fit us

instead of us fitting it.

I am the space between atoms

The warmth between your thighs

The goosebumps running down your back and

Your chest when you breathe in and rise.

It was for more than just a taste

To satisfy a deep hunger

That feeling of chilli and hot chocolate

Sweet and tingling you want it to stay longer –

and

This is euphoria.

There are no barriers

No signs of

"Do not trespass".

Like the opening night of a long-anticipated theatre

Every fibre of your being is here

Right here

Right now.

Euphoria surpasses happiness

And sits deeply beyond mind and heart.

Ocean waves crashing into icebergs and volcanic caves -

That is to say,

everything connects and in this moment,

this moment there is no beginning or end

The fountain overflows with water.

How can I accurately describe something so climactic?

In this suspended time, you are a galaxy.

You are every speck of dust, every star and solar system.

You feel it all as a rush through your very core

And this is euphoria.

Clear blue skies but darkly rung eyes

Skin stretched across bone frame crawls

The energy seeping out is ghostly and untouchable

The stench crosses fence lines.

Coloured blue is the ocean and the sky the same but untrue

A grin from ear to ear stretched by barbs on fishhooks

Silence is loudest at 5am

Did you hear the white wall scream?

A cat who prowls on frowning owls

Minds set to a timer for destruction

Connecting the dots is making the ugliest of pictures

Blissful ignorance would be welcome here.

As hot water runs cold time becomes old

Racing hearts come to grinding and sudden holts

The dust settles after the tornado

This might not have ended with optimism.

Rise like the sun on a cold foggy morning

Shining on the dew swept grass, turning the cool breeze warm.

Rise because you are inevitable.

Each day is new.

Each moment a fresh opportunity to see the flower buds open, honour the permanently sleeping, and move a little closer to what makes your insides buzz with excitement.

The inevitable rise comes before the inevitable setting.

As the light shines bright and the skies turn orange, pink, and purple

Tonight you can rest easy and rebuild your strength.

Maybe I didn't want to die,

I just didn't want to live

Like this.

When death becomes a glowing warm exit instead of a warning
sign

It does not mean this is where the story is supposed to finish –

It means something needs to change

Something to make your eyes bright, muscles relax and heart soar.

I'm terrified of living,

and I'm terrified of missing the little moments where a graze of my
skin on theirs gives me goosebumps,

how my cat purring vibrates through my body as he sleeps on my
chest,

seeing the world in colour

instead of tones of grey.

The colour might be turned down or off at times,

but no feeling lasts forever.

As I experience sadness, aching and pain as waves crashing against the rocks on the cliffs edge,

so too can I experience the happiness, joys and comfort of the waves gently lapping the shore.

And without the waves of sadness, how could I ever know and appreciate the happiness?

That is not to say I'm grateful for my pain -

but that it makes me value the little moments so much more.

I live for every smile of those around me that I feel to my very core,

for the infinite shades of green in every leaf and blade of grass,

The way the forest smells after the rain and the birds sing in the treetops,

and every pitter patter of love I share with another.

I may not always feel pleasure

And the exit sign might glow.

But I hold on for me;

for the oceans to calm,

my atoms to respond to theirs,

and the knowledge that just as the exit sign lights up

I can find the switch to turn it off.

I know all the patterns of the pavement

But so little of the skyline.

You think this is a metaphor, but it isn't,

I can't look up.

Deep exhale when I walk on perfectly smooth cement or
wonderfully soft grass

Followed by short sharp breaths and tense muscles as I try to
navigate squares or varying colours, shapes and sizes while trying
not to fall over.

If you want to see a sober person look drunk while walking, look -

I am right here.

I am not afraid of snakes or lizards,

Spiders make my skin crawl

But birds, worms, rats and mice

Please let me hold you and love you.

Cliff edges, deep diving, abseiling, cave exploring and swimming with sharks I excitedly sit with anticipation to experience.

I wish I were joking when I said the one thing that inhibits my ability to physically move around this earth...is lines and cracks in pavement.

The disorganisation of uneven footsteps holds such internal chaos the world suddenly feels dangerous and chaotic.

I would rather sit in a pit of snakes than step on the lines of tiny squares on a bathroom floor.

18

I imagine death not as a warm embrace of past lives lived

But as the cool air on a winters morning when I open the window and let the morning light shine in.

That is what I imagine.

More accurately it's the cool air on a winter's morning gripping my throat so tightly I begin to suffocate infinitely –

The sun shines through the open window but it is hollow and offers no comfort.

The truth is when I am depressed death seems a kindness and it isn't just for me

It is for everyone around me.

How painful it must be to watch bones crack at the wrong angles and know there is nothing you can do to prevent the pain the other person is going through.

Together in pain, yet such different experiences of hopelessness and

helplessness.

One desperate for it to just end any way possible,

the other pleading with the shadows to loosen their grip and return

the person they love.

Living is terrifying.

So many ways to experience pain, suffering and misery...

Death may release that pressure but oh god,

so too does it remove the possibility for unspeakable pleasure,

laughter, and love.

I am not going to live for other people.

I am going to live to witness the flowers bloom,

to hold the ones I love and hear their stories,

experience the satisfaction of completing my new favourite book.

Death is the cold shadow tapping on my shoulder,

But life?

Life is the sunrise pouring through the window and warming my cheeks and heart.

Open the window.

"No" is a complete sentence.

You do not owe anyone an explanation or justification for asserting your boundaries.

"No" is a complete sentence while

"Yes" is holding a semi colon

Ready to withdraw when needed, conditional.

Say "No" and nothing more.

Say "Yes" and remember your limits.

Look me in the eyes and call me by my name.

Remember when there is a fork in the road,

I choose my way

Or forge a new path never walked before.

Run your fingers through my hair and let the breeze blow gently on my skin.

I am the ease of a gentle rainforest walk and

The power of one thousand suns together.

Where I stand there is no shadow.

I am tall and I stand strong,

I radiate light.

Standing in my shower,

The sound of each droplet of water encompasses me.

Steam fills the air.

I wrap myself in my towel, soft

And move to the mirror.

I stand in front of the fogged-up mirror

This speech is for no one else.

Wipe the mirror gently and put my shoulders back as I inhale and repeat again -

Look me in the eyes and call me by my name.